ROBERT

WAITING
FOR THE WAVE

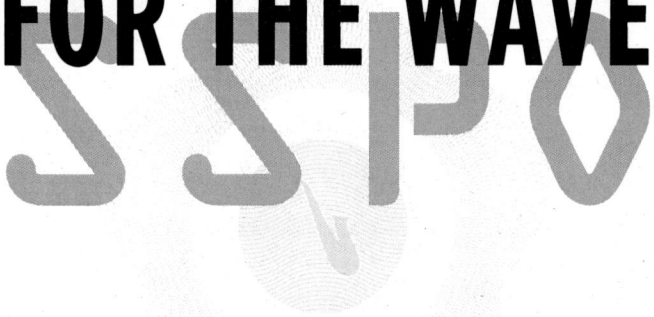

Design by Aneel Kalsi

ISBN 978-1-906309-19-0

First published June 2012 by
Pighog Press
PO Box 145
Brighton BN1 6YU
England UK

info@pighog.co.uk
www.pighog.co.uk
www.facebook.com/Pighog
@Pighog

CONTENTS

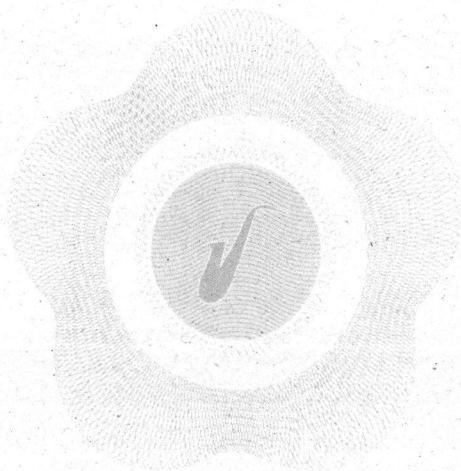

J'ai toujours aimé le desert.
On s'assoit sur une dune de sable.
On ne voit rien. On n'entend rien.
Et cependant quelque chose rayonne en silence...

'Le Petit Prince' – Antoine de St-Exupéry

FOR CAROL

PILLBOX

Twenty thousand dawns I've watched
The shudder of light on the meandering waters,
The reeds on standby for the valley's invasions.

Waiting for the drone of raiding aircraft,
I've only spotted the hawk high over Hindover,
Hanging its threat from an invisible tripwire.

Listening for the boom on the foreshore, the thud
Between the breaking waves, I've only heard
The landing-craft of swans cruising upstream.

Watching for the shadow on the hills, the dark cross
Slipping in and out of cloud, I've only glimpsed
A glint of heron's beak, lone sniper in the reeds.

Twenty thousand dawns I've waited:
Wind in the hawthorn, elder, chestnut;
Light shaking the cowslips, trembling the silverweed.

TRIANGULATION

Introduction

Come with us now, beyond this enclosure of calm water, its surface
shimmering between the basin walls, beneath the crescents
banking up through Clifton Wood to Royal York's silhouette,

come out to the wedge of land bevelling the mudbanks,
this triangulation of waterways where Avon, New Cut
and Floating Harbour meet, to take the measure of time:

down the centuries, sail and timber have held the sway,
the vessels riding the tide from Portbury, ready to discharge
their cargoes from Riga, Mauritius, Madras and Quebec;

West African hardwood, beeswax, copal gum and palm-oil;
plantation sugar from Guyana and Barbados; oranges and citrus
ripe from the Azores; from Oporto, sacks of nuts, barrels of wine.

But for the present, the future lies in iron and steam
– forged in the furnace, driven by piston and valve -
and all beyond is the construction of calculation and vision.

I Brunel Lock

Here, the gathering of water. First, the levelling of surfaces,
the inflow rising inch by gurgling inch from harbour to reservoir,
settling to stillness at a point of perfect balance -

the water, like polished brass, held within the granite quoins
and copings of this quiet chamber, its wrought-iron caisson gates
on shutting-pieces of finest mahogany, closing the reach

from Cumberland to Netham. All along the wharves,
the schooners, packets, cutters, trows and brigs sit moored
at Mardyke and Limekiln up to Wapping and Canon's Marsh

- 'Minerva', 'Magic', 'Velox', 'Dispatch', 'Levant' and 'Mars',
'United Friends', 'Sybilla', 'Vintage', 'Orestes', 'Rapid',
grand 'Augusta' and 'William Miles' Tobago bound -

designed, built, rigged and launched in the quayside yards
of Stothert, Hilhouse, Acramans, Green and Hill — tonight,
their topmasts starlit, figureheads gleaming, they wait on the tide:

in a tracery of booms and spars, mizzens, mains and cables,
stays and derricks soaring skyward, sounding the fathoms,
they sway to the slightest ruffle of sou' westerly wind -

until one by one they creak and groan downstream to the Basin
where each will drift between these iron arms, loosely tethered,
as the keepers turn the windlass, link by link, to close the paddles

while the ships lie there easily, waiting to glide out into the Gorge
from this gathering of water he stuck out for, argued,
bargained and fought for, this entrance and outlet to the world.

II Swingbridge

Between this quay and that quay, that side and this,
the channel we cannot stride across, the drop, the plunge,

the absence of uplift, where gravity's downward pressure
pulls you towards the surface to wrap you in its depths

should you step beyond these granite blocks, this warning line,
this edge of emptiness wide as fear can stretch.

To carry the traffic of feet and wheels and so much tonnage
trundling the empire's trade and plunder back and forth,

the passage of officers and mariners, the merchants haggling delivery
with hauliers, the press of militia, journeymen in their gangs,

carriages clattering, wagons and drays rolling, the clunk
of horses and livestock, the clutter of jetty lumber and chandlery—

it needs not just a structure to bear the weight, but demands both
the imagination's aspiration to leap boundlessly into air

and the equipoise of function, material and design, engineered
to the phenomenon of the place, an arc to join this quay to that.

So here it is, his prototype bridge of riveted tubular girders,
its tail-end wheels askew, its roller-rails awry,

turntable seized up on its mechanism and chains. Dry-docked
in the cradle of flyover and sliproad. From its rusting flanges,

sprigs of buddleia sprout, while along its deck, like the ghost
of a sailor, a moth in the lamplight dances a hornpipe.

III   Underfall Sluice

In Jessop's crowded Harbour, the Overfall into the Cut,
a tumble of water spinning its loom over the weir.
Yet up to the brink, almost imperceptible in its constant motion,

the surface glinted, now here, now there, from grey dawn
to phosphorescent dusk. Its mirror images of the vessels,
their fabulous figureheads, sleek hulls and galleries,

replicated in shadow and reflection, and little more
than a long arc of ripple where the flatness fell away.
He knew that damming the flow from the Float to the Cut

would not disturb the silt shoaling on the harbour bed,
the deposits clogging the channels of passage,
nuzzling and crusting the keels. He knew

the power of the undercurrent, its fierce charge driven
by the hydraulic force of trunk and culvert. He knew
an underfall's undertow would draw the silt down the syphon

and thrust it out into the draining tide. Below the surface,
the daily turbulence scoured the dock walls clean -
filtration, dispersal, release. And so it proves still.

When the warning lights flash red in the Harbourmaster's Yard,
you can feel the subterranean pull through the wells below,
beneath the Sluice House the cast-iron paddles churning.

Cross the Cumberland Road to the towpath to watch the outflow
pouring into the ebb and rapids, and where the broken water
is running, a cormorant dives against the tide, comes up gleaming.

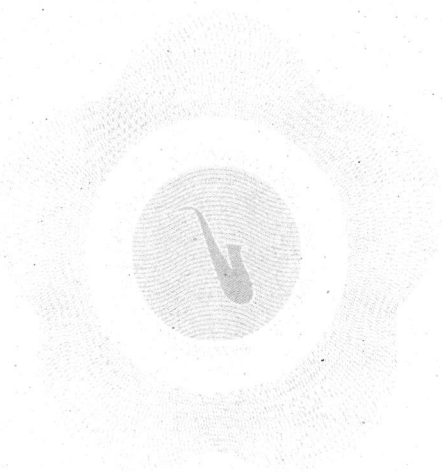

SURF

I

out the back
    beyond the surge and race
        of the white waters
            where the scrambling shallows
                churn and scour the shoreline
          beyond
              the slow elevation
                the
              sudden plunge
                  and crash
                    and the spindrift flying

I wait
on the board
between
the blue   and   the blue
suspended
between the ocean's turbine swell
and the shimmering air
defined
by undulant horizons

I wait
on firewatch
as the sets
arrive

on a roll
smouldering
from open sea

like blue combustible mountains
range upon range

I wait
perched on the board
raptor in the treetops
speculating upon the specific

- the spotting
the stoop
the strike

waiting
for
the wave

II

Reef-cruiser, sandbank-seether risen from the depths,
        it rears its glossy dorsal, turns the surface
of the underocean over. Silver-glazed leviathan,
        the offshore winds scroll its crest to perfection.

I stretch along the deck, seated in the channel
        like a pilot in the cockpit, tripswitched to the countdown.
And as the face peaks to the break, I launch
        below the lip-curl and chute into the tube.

        I ride the geodesic line
                inside a dome of molten glass,
        at equipoise on the wheel of time
                this white-hot moment's dynamic force

                I am porpoise, I am shark
                I am dolphin, I am seal

        I ride the radiance of the crystal sphere
                like Jonah's jive in the belly of the whale,
        a silent music resonant in my ears
                I dance to the vibe of its breaking scale

                I am porpoise, I am shark
                I am dolphin, I am seal

III

And out onto the shoulder
                    into the light
                            into the air
        bottom-turn
                cutback
                    floater
                        re-o
                            and hang ten
out on the gleaming wave
                        fins shooting spray
            until the board bucks
            and nosedives
                and I eject
                    freefall
                        freefall
                            freefall
                                into
                                    the shredding surf

COASTAL

Momentarily the landmarks confuse: those steps
        could be the stile; tracks in the grass imply
a right of way in both directions. In a flap
        of wind, the map wriggles and tugs in his hand.

There's time to take in the day's brilliance. Turning,
        she watches the slant of light, its needlepoints
piercing the clouds to trim the waves with lacework
        where the sea scoops and folds on the rocks below

Contours blur. The dotted routes converge
        with boundaries. Glancing up, now staring
down, he fits the symbols to the lie of the land.
        Sees the gap. Resolved, he steps it out.

Holding her ground on the headland, she hears the cry
        of a windward bird, hanging somewhere out there
below the edge. And still the waves surge
        towards her, booming through some hidden blowhole.

SAX BURGLAR BLUES

As he crept through the darkness to ease
                    you from the stand where you sat
like a swan in the reeds – could he hear
                    your stabs and riffs, fierce
and rhythmic as wings beating the waters,
                    rising into the groove of the air?

And when he touched you, hand-in-glove
                    fumbling your gleaming mechanisms,
your keys clumping in his grasp
                    - did he hear your screech
of protest, the upper octave alarm
                    of a hawk squalling on the leash?

He took you apart. Dismantled note
                    from note your smooth arpeggios,
your bebop solos. Squeezed the bell
                    beneath his arm. Twisted
out the crook. Slipped the mouthpiece
                    from the cork. And stooping

to zip you piece by piece into the bag,
                    did he share the night-owl
haunts of your rambling blues? Could he
                    imagine your bottom B flat,
profound and plaintive enough to rouse
                    a seal from the ocean depths?

UP THE BLUEBIRDS!

for my father

Season on season, week on week,
your irrepressible optimism on the phone:
down the line I hear the chant
of the home crowd, see the pitch
where the ball arcs between boot and upright
or hangs in the wind over upturned heads.
And yes, I try to share that surge
of joy as the net bulges and you leap
from your seat, arms upthrust, to roar
for the goals that justify your lifelong fervour.

Week in week out, each word you speak –
the keeper's saves, the striker's misses,
the names of players I've never heard of,
the tactics, the ref's outrageous decisions –
spins from your mouth like a string
of bright rosettes in some conjuring trick.
I listen, ask questions, enthuse.
Somewhere in a wardrobe in my house
a Bluebirds scarf, bought years ago outside
the ground, lies folded in the dark.

COUSIN

In Aunty Dot's kitchen, you lay in ambush
on the table, watched me crawl between the legs
and clamber upright clutching the oilcloth,
before you struck. Pummelling my Dumpty head,
your giant rubber mallet squealed with delight.

And months later, I turned to catch your grin
as you waved from the doorstep squeezing a neighbour's
hand, while Aunty Dot nursed me to the taxi.
A perfect fit, you'd said, poking the peas
up my nostrils, your forefinger prodding them home.

Scrambling over the fence, we'd chase a zigzag
through the fields to race up Red Canyon.
When I reached the top, you were always waiting,
laughing as you stamped on my fingers and rolled me
back down in the dust, your victory yell echoing.

The tales have long settled into family lore,
your genial mischief. Today the news comes through.
A shiver of silence down the line: I picture you
icing up in your chair as the days freeze
around you, little doll with a glazed stare.

OCCASION

Easing your hand
sideways-on
between the raspy
canes and into
the canopy of pale
green light

you twist and lift
your wrist beneath
the curling, curative
trusses of leaves
as if practising
a magician's gesture

in search of rubus
idaeus - as Ida
did for infant Zeus,
the drops of blood
from her pricked breast
soaking the white berries

forever red -
as now, with palm
cupped, closing
your finger-tips
round the ruby
drupelets, you pull

away, unhasping
the fruit from its plug,
the rich juices
drizzling your skin
with the same traces
which, offered up,

imprint my lips,
sweet on the tongue.

SNOWWOMAN

Just there, between the snowcapped posts at the end of the path,
the first compacted handful, moulded in the gloves

then rolled and rolled around again in the scrunchy stuff,
becomes a pediment, half-sunk it seems, at the chosen spot.

How soon the base widens: ball on ball compressed
into place. It feels like the day of creation, for still the soft

flakes fall, hither and thither, adrift in the playful air,
as the torso rises, rounding up towards the shoulder's

cold command. It stands alone. Bluestone menhir
in early light, its mystery crystallising the moment.

Now for the head. It takes an eye to judge the fit,
cupping it out of the snow - a crown found in treasure-hoard -

and lifting it up to sit at the neckless juncture. Eyeless,
she takes it all in. Mouthless, her silence tells all. Made.

NOMAD '64   i.m. Don Cherry 1936 - 1995

1.   Touchdown

Down the flightpath from Manhattan to Morocco
                    the glinting fuselage threads the sun's last rays
cloth of gold of ocean and sky.

And the man in the beret in the window-seat
                    watches   beyond the wing-tip
                            horizons shift and fall.
                                    In prisms of fading light
                            he hears   beneath the engine's thrum
                    the rhythms of the ancient world,
                            the language of the tribes.

Lodged in the luggage-rack,
           compact amongst the coats
and packages, the black case sits.
                    Inside,
sleek as antlers in its velvet wrap,
                    the trumpet gleams:
coiled fossil   horn of Jupiter
           in its subterranean bed.
Bell, valves, mouthpiece
                - mute molluscs,
                    pearls cultured
in the man's atlantean imagination.

Touchdown. The retros screech, snarl
                    the jetstreams. Wheels thunder down the
runway
                         like the drum of blood in the ears.
Wings and tail-fin scythe the dusk,
                    sharking across the apron
                         to a halt.

First steps onto Africa, a shiver of dust at his heels,
                the air warm and sweet as molasses.
He carries the case like a conch, an offering
                    on his arrival   his homecoming.

2.   Djemma El Fna

In Djemma el Fna, the kerosene-lamps glow
                    Shadows crowd the smoke-plumes
                              Phantoming the square.
The man with the trumpet by the Café de France
                    Listens to the babble in the nomadic air

                    Storytellers jabber
                              Watersellers chant
                    Tarot-readers whisper
                              Preachers rant

          The orange-juice vendor juggles his fruit
          A carpet-merchant brags of the rugs at his feet
          The snake-charmer's pipe weaves its mystic sound
          A grinning beggar offers his arthritic hand

          Acrobats and drummers
          Dancers, comedians, clowns
          Perform their rituals, spellbind the crowd
          Herbalists and dentists
          Apothecaries, scribes
          Concoct in the darkness the magic of the tribe

          Down from the Atlas
          The Berbers flock
          Through the gateways and the alleys
          To the markets and the souks
          Sheepskins, kaftans, incense, jewels
          They trade their wares, their perfumes and oils
          For the dirham, the dollar, the franc or the mark
          The bartered deal is their ancient art

The Eastern star sparkles beyond the minaret –
          The man with the trumpet explores the citadel:

Ramparts, palaces, mosques and a courtyard
            Where a fountain scintillates amongst the lemon-trees.
On a breath of wind that riffles the palm-leaves
He hears the rage and rumble of distant cities

            In New York and Cleveland
            The student boycott's called
            'No segregation in education!
            Demand the right to be enrolled!'
            X is on the platform, Jackson's in San Quentin
            Riots on the streets in Harlem and Brooklyn
            Luther King's dream is last year's news
            The prophet on the mountain's dazzled by the views

            Looting and shooting
            Ransacked offices and shops
            Overturned sedans
            Molotovs for the cops
            Hydrants leap and roar like dragons in the sky
            Sirens scream and wail their frantic cry
            The ghettoes of America give the rainbow-sign
            No more water, the fire next time

No more water
                        The fire next time

            No more water
                        The fire next time

In Marrakech and New York the night-lamps glow
            Shadows crowd the smoke-plumes
                        Phantoming the square

The man with the trumpet and iced coke by the Café de France
            Listens to the babble of the arabesque air

3.   Sahara

Moonlit silhouette on the dune-crest,
        the trumpet sits at his lips
- compass-needle poised to the earth's tilt,
           weather-vane-swivel on the desert's breath.

Wind-fluted   lunar sandscape
       sun-scorched   vulture-haunt

His notes leap and flare
        amethyst glissando quavering the air
and the stars crackle
             from the silver horn
                blue acetylene-sparks
welding arpeggio constellations
               in the firefly dark.

Sahara scrubland   snake-hide
       rock-strewn Mahgreb   lizard-perch

He holds the trumpet like a divining-rod
        tuned to the elemental pull:
the slightest shimmer of sand
        is the rippled surface of an oasis-pool,
the merest stir of air
        a stifled sigh   a whispered breath
is the wave-lace woven on a distant shore.

4.   ESSAOUIRA

The sea at Essaouira lifts
             and settles in a muted dawn
like the breath of a sleeper
             in a wilderness of dreams.

Astir on the horizon,
             the sun is a bloodshot eye:
it flickers, blinks, opens
             in a pale-skinned sky.

He stands at the edge of the quay,
             catches the breeze in the sails
of his mind; and the waves' pulse
             plays on the rigging of the stave.

History's the key to which he ties his tune.

    And the gulls screech in the sardine-boats' wake ...

        The gulls screech in the sardine-boats' wake ...

           The gulls screech in the sardine-boats' wake.

5.   DEPARTURE

The man with the foot-soles of wind
hangs around in the departure lounge.
Transglobal lassitude hums in the air,
mid-day suspension of the hypnotised senses.

Duty-free browsers in a perfumed drowse,
cabin-crews glossy and glassy-eyed as dolls,
customs-officials stern as filing-cabinets,
armed police twitching their cigarettes
                    like triggers,
and the thousand terminal passengers,
hooded, hunched, slumped and slouched
beneath the clicking information-displays.

And there, the black case cradled
like a rocket-launcher in his lap,
 he scans through burning tinted glass
the ever-open skies and his mind

is air-borne

                    towards

                                        The Five Spot

Albert Ayler
Sonny Rollins
John Coltrane

                    they got the blues

Archie Shepp
Dexter Gordon
Gato Barbieri

                    they got the blues

Ed Blackwell
Charlie Haden
Ornette Coleman

          they got the blues .

Don Byas
Carla Bley
Billy Higgins

          they got the blues

George Russell
Clifford Brown
Miles Davis

          they got the blues

Colin Walcott
Nana Vasconcelos
Han Bennink

          they got the blues

Steve Lacey
Dewey Redman
Red Mitchell
Eric Dolphy
Freddie Hubbard
Scott La Faro

          they got the blues

Thundering down the runway, the names race
like blood in the ears.

          Lift.

              Take off.

NOTES

Pillbox: Written when I was a member of Footwork,
a collective of Sussex poets. This was for a poetry-walk along
the valley at Cuckmere Haven. It was read from inside a
pillbox on the hillside, catching the audience unawares on
the footpath below.

Triangulation: Written for the Brunel 200 Celebrations in
Bristol, 2006. It was presented with music composed by Pete
Judge and visual projections and film by Reuben Knutsen on
the evening of Sunday 8 April underneath the Cumberland
Basin flyovers.

Surf: Written to be performed with music composed by
Pete Judge and the band, mopti, it celebrates my discovery
of and fantasies about surfing in Australia.

Nomad '64:   Written in memory of the great jazz trumpeter
and musical innovator, Don Cherry. The piece was performed
with music composed by Pete Judge and the band mopti –
trumpet, guitar, bass, percussion. It was recorded and released
on cd by writtenonwater.

Born and brought up in Cardiff, Robert studied English Literature at Exeter University. In 1978 his first collection, 'Workings', won the Welsh Arts Council's New Poet Award. Strangely (and he still doesn't understand why) he immediately stopped writing. It wasn't until the 90s that he resumed. Since then he has written poems for performance in collaboration with musicians, artists, dancers, film-makers and storytellers. A founder member of the Sussex poetry collective, Footwork, he wrote the poetry script for the drama-documentary about Alfred Sisley, 'Fighting to the End' (dir. Colin Thomas, BBC2 Wales, 2008). He has had six monologues produced by Bristol's Show of Strength Theatre Company. After a career as an English teacher, he gained an MA with distinction in Creative Writing at Cardiff University in 2011 and is now a working towards his PhD.